Junior Science
floating and sinking

Terry Jennings

Illustrations by David Anstey

Gloucester Press
New York · London · Toronto · Sydney

About this book

You can learn all about floating and sinking in this book. There are many different experiments for you to try. You will find out why some things float but others sink, how important air is to floating and sinking, how to make a stone float, how to make a small sailing boat and much more.

First published in the
United States in 1988 by
Gloucester Press
387 Park Avenue South
New York, NY 10016

ISBN 0 531 17086 1

Library of Congress Catalog
Card Number: 87-82972

© BLA Publishing Limited 1988

This book was designed and produced by BLA Publishing Limited, TR House, Christopher Road, East Grinstead, Sussex, England.

A member of the Ling Kee Group
London Hong Kong Taipei Singapore New York
Printed in Spain by Heraclio Fournier, S.A.

J532.2 J448
Jennings, Terry
Floating and sinking
9.90

3 0000 10061236 9

DATE DUE

THIS BOOK WITHDRAWN FROM
THE RECORDS OF THE
MID-CONTINENT PUBLIC LIBRARY

SEP 17 2003

MID-CONTINENT PUBLIC LIBRARY

Platte City
320 Main
Platte City, Mo. 64079

PC

Books circulate for four weeks (28 days) unless stamped otherwise.

No renewals are allowed.

Books will be issued only on presentation of library card.

A fine will be charged for each overdue book.

Some things float and some things sink in water. Collect different objects like these in the picture. Fill a large bowl with water and put them in the bowl one at a time.

Floats	Sinks
Cork	Small stone

See whether they will float or sink. You can make two lists like this.

Here are some things which will float and some things which sink. Each heap weighs 5 ounces. But they are not all the same size. The heaps of materials which float are larger than those which sink.

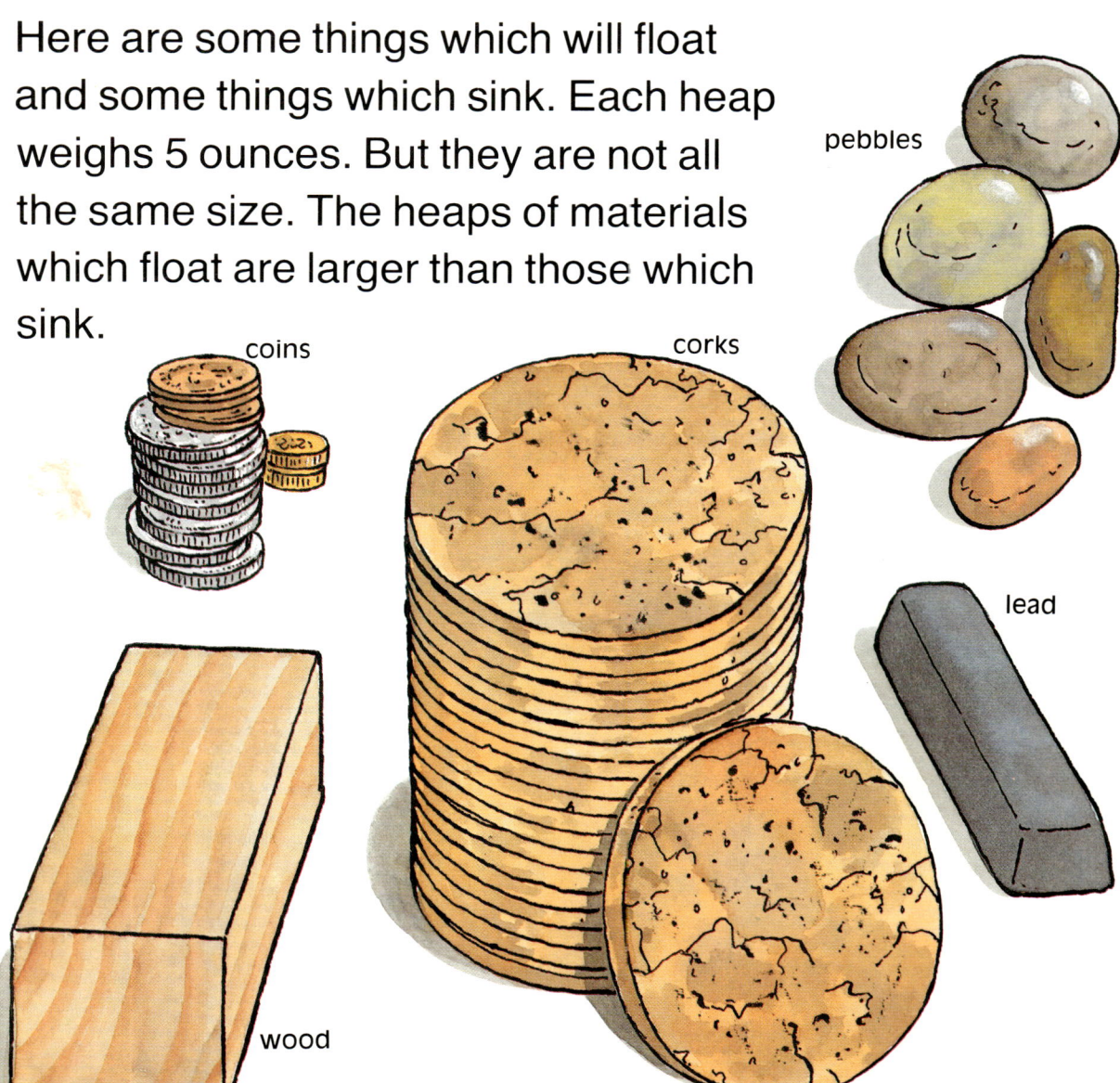

Put a bottle top in water and you will see that it floats. Ask a grown-up to help you crush it into a solid ball. The bottle top will sink. It still weighs the same but it now takes up a much smaller space.

Roll out some modeling clay until it is thin. Make a boat shape with the modeling clay and put it into a bowl of water. The boat will float. Now take the boat out of the water and roll it into a ball. The ball of modeling clay will sink because it now takes up a much smaller space.

A big ship is very heavy. It is made of steel. If the ship were made into a solid ball of steel it would sink. Steel ships float because the metal is shaped so that there is lots of air inside.

Float an empty can in a bowl of water. Mark the water level on the bowl and on the can. If you put a disk of modeling clay in the can it will float deeper in the water. The water level in the bowl will be higher because the can is pushing more water out of the way. If you put more modeling clay in the can the water may come over the top and it will sink.

You might have seen ships like this in a harbor. There are lots of big boxes on the ship at the top. The ship at the bottom has unloaded the boxes. Look how the empty ship floats much higher in the water.

Air helps objects to float. Here are four glass bottles all of the same size. There is water in three of the bottles. Three bottles have air in them. One bottle has only water.

The three bottles with air in them will float. The empty bottle will float highest in the water. The bottle full of water will sink.

Take two empty cans. Fill one with water and put them both in a bowl of water. The can which is full of water will sink. The other can will float. If you sink the empty can you will see air bubbles as it fills with water. This shows that the can was not really empty. It was filled with air.

Put a tennis ball in a bucket of water and you will see that the ball floats. If you push the tennis ball under the water it will seem as if the water is pushing the ball up. When you let go the ball will bob to the surface again.

If you push a soccer ball under the water, you will have to push harder. This is because the soccer ball is bigger. It has to push much more water out of the way.

You can make a stone float! Take an empty plastic bottle with a cap and put it in water. It will float. Put a small stone in the water and of course it will sink.

Now tie the stone to the plastic bottle. The bottle will hold the stone up in the water. You could use any large air-filled object to make a small heavy object float.

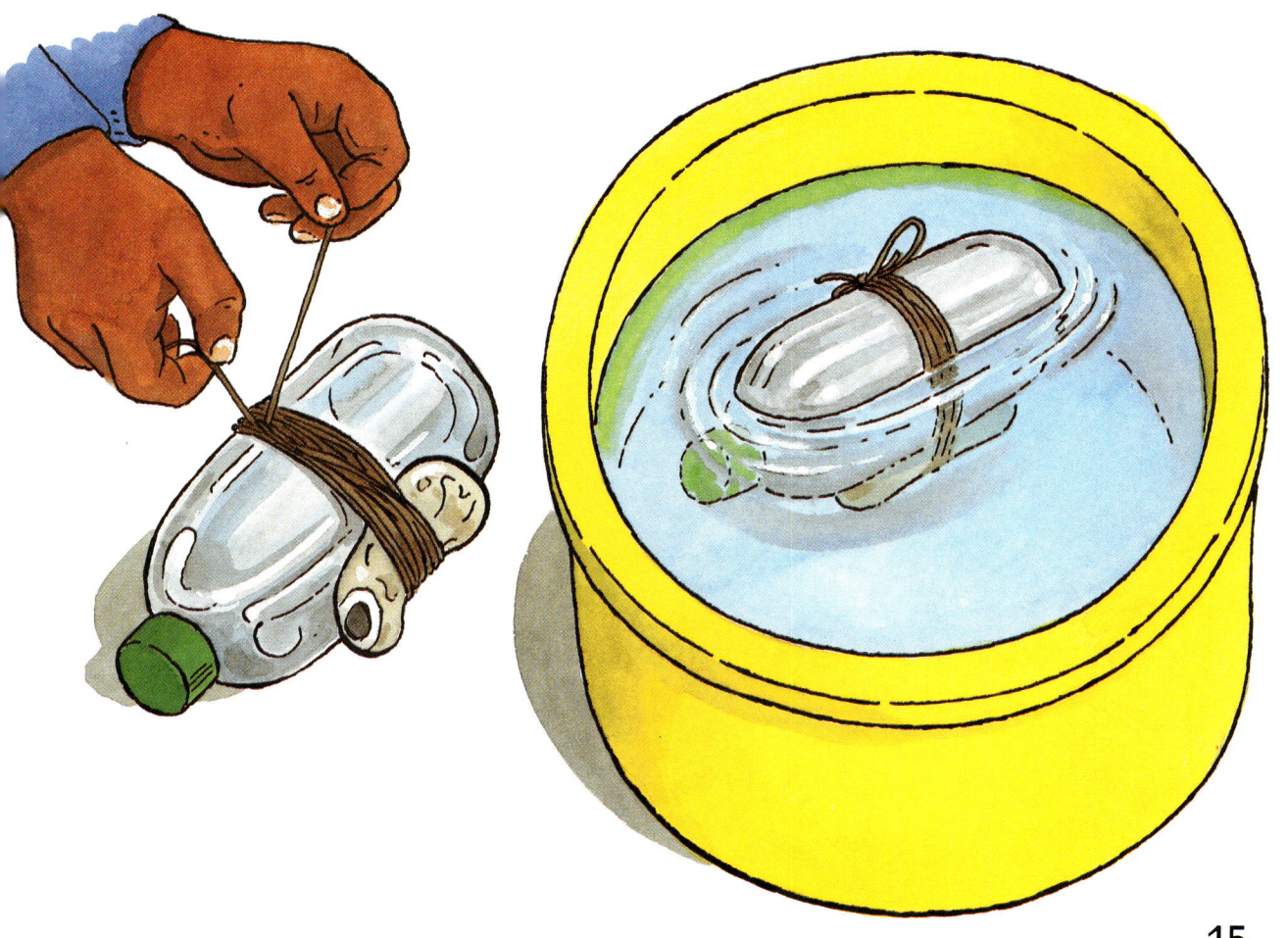

Perhaps you have used water wings at a swimming pool. Many people cannot make themselves float when they are learning to swim. If they wear water wings which are filled with air it becomes much easier to float.

An iceberg is a big lump of ice floating in the sea. Icebergs form where it is very cold. About one-eighth of the iceberg is above the water. About seven-eighths of the iceberg is below the water. So the iceberg looks smaller than it really is.

A cork floats high in the water. An iceberg floats low. In the picture there are four different blocks of wood which are all the same size. When the blocks are put in water they all float. But some float higher than others. The balsa wood block floats high. The oak block floats low.

Salt water helps things to float. If something floats low in tap water, it will float higher in salt water. A sea called the Dead Sea is the most salty sea in the world. It is so salty that people can float easily in it.

Take a block of wood and put it in a bowl of tap water. Add lots of salt and the block of wood will float higher.

You can make a sailing boat from a matchbox. Put a small piece of modeling clay in the matchbox. Cut out a square of paper and push it onto a cocktail stick. This is the sail.
Push the sail into the modeling clay.

Now take an empty detergent bottle. Put your boat on a bowl of water and squeeze the bottle at the sail of the boat. Air will rush out of the bottle and push the sailing boat along.

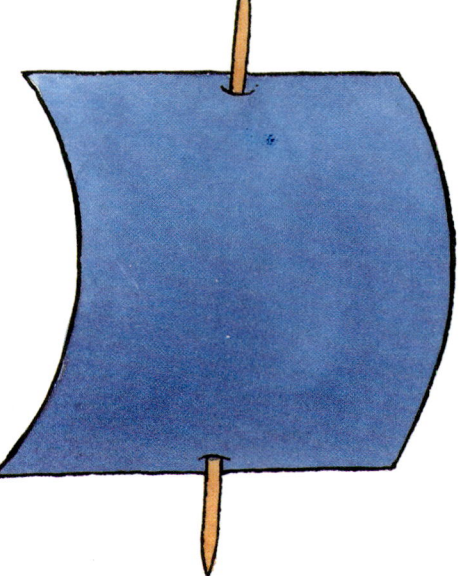

If you put sand in a jar of water it will sink to the bottom. If you put small pieces of cork into the jar they will float. To separate the sand and cork scoop the cork off the surface of the water. Then carefully tip the water away and the sand will be left in the bottom of the jar.

glossary

Here are the meanings of some words you may have used for the first time in this book.

disk: anything flat and circular in shape.

float: to stay on the surface of water or another liquid.

iceberg: a large lump of ice floating in the sea.

sink: to go down into water or another liquid.

steel: a strong metal made from iron.

water wings: air-filled floats which can be fixed to the arms of someone learning to swim.

index

air 7, 10, 11, 15, 16, 20
boats and ships 6, 7, 9, 20
coins 4
cork 3, 4, 18, 22
Dead Sea 19
iceberg 17, 18, 23
lead 4
modeling clay 6, 8, 20
salt 19

sand 22
size 4, 5, 6
steel 7, 23
stones 3, 4, 14, 15
swimming 16
water level 8
water wings 16, 23
weight 4, 5
wood 4, 18, 19